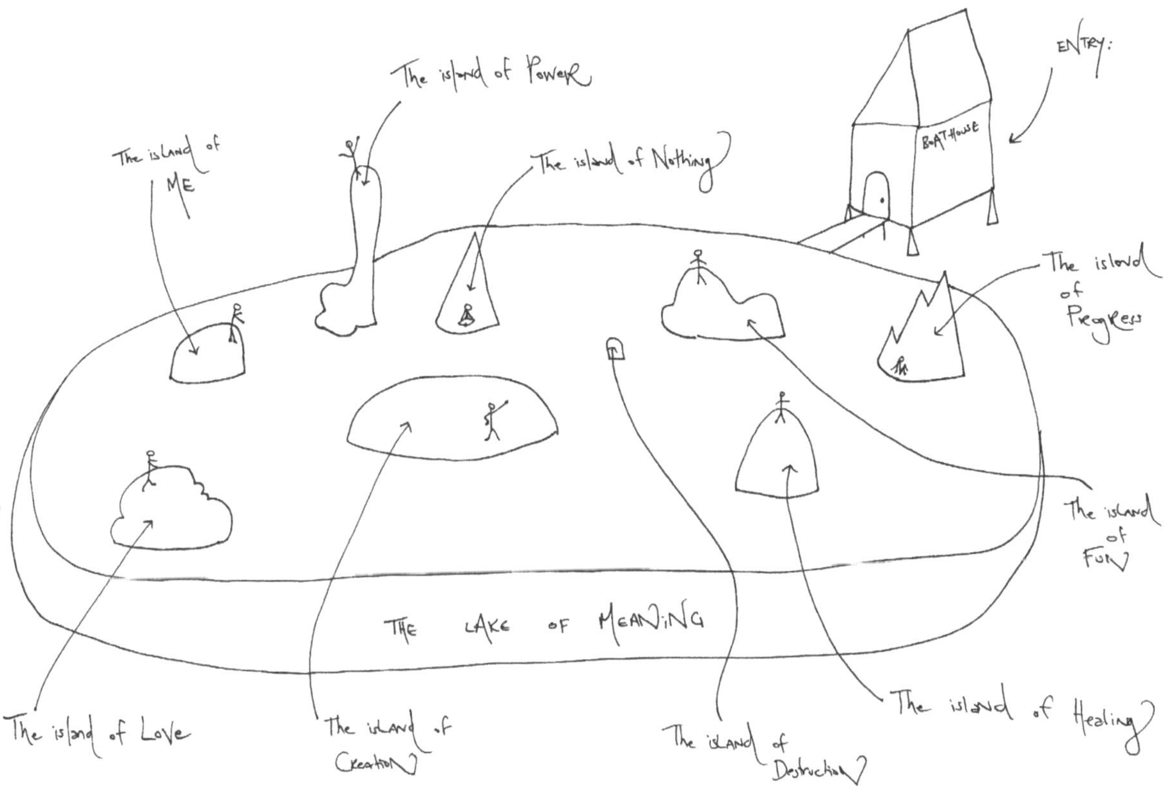

*We keep memories of what we looked like in photograph albums … But where
do we keep the memories of what we were thinking at the time? Please keep your
thoughts in these books as if they were your own journals. Or cut them up and sticky
tape them into something else, to keep memories of your mind forevermore.*

Other books in the Young Philosophers series

The Book With No Story
The Fake Dictionary
The One Thing And Anothers

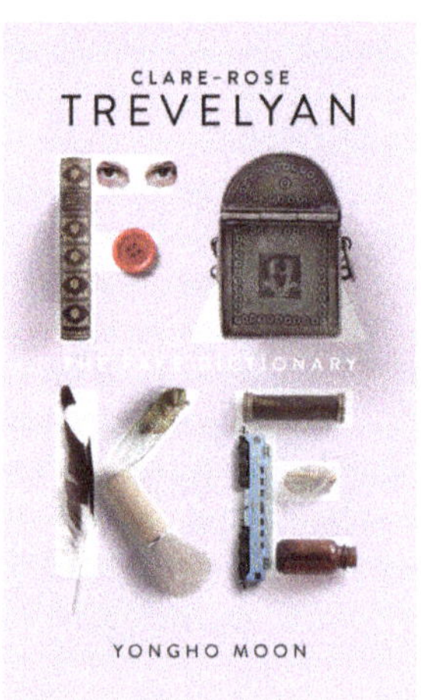

Other books in the Past Life Library novella series
with accompanying soundtracks

Eternal Inka
Everlasting Charli
Infinite Aisa
Forever Raphaella
Always Rose

CLARE-ROSE TREVELYAN

WHY IN THE WORLD ARE WE HERE

Young Philosophers Series Vol. 3
A Whereabouts of Wanderings

HOW TO USE THIS BOOK

1.

Read the story and keep in mind questions about the
meaning of your life, what matters to you and exactly
how you'd like to live your own life.

2.

Choose your favourite island as if you yourself were
paddling around a huge LAKE in a theme park and
choosing where you would live of all the places.
Keep all your thoughts in a journal.

3.

Go to the back of the book to make your own island,
complete with law, currency, a motto, flag and a historic
story of how your island came to be.

4.

Create as many islands or places within your island as
you like, and you perhaps may start to wonder about
who in your life would live on which island, or wonder
about if life itself has any meaning at all, or if indeed
perhaps you are to make up your own meaning?

WHY IN THE WORLD ARE WE HERE

6

Away in the future when my name was Eia and I lived with my best friend Whhat on our glipperty-boomp island, we would sit together and wonder.

It was a beautiful island. The moon-suns passed in the clouds above and the no-name creatures swam in the waters below. Whhat and I never did anything except endlessly wonder why in the world we were here.

We would think and think and think and think … but we would never find the answer.

Beneath the moon-suns we sat, as confused as we had always been.

One day I got so fed up with thinking that I lost my temper.

"I'm sick and tired of trying to figure it out!" I snapped at Whhat. Whhat blinked, startled. "We must go and find out why in the world we are here before we both go completely mad!" I angrily commanded, and I began stamping off toward a raft we had made a few years back but had never yet used.

"OK," shrugged Whhat, and she followed.

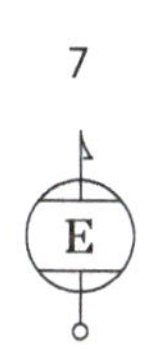

The sea was calm and it whispered to us in a language we couldn't understand. After many moon-suns passed, Whhat saw something in the distance. She whipped out her kaleidoscope.

"Look!" she shouted and pointed.

"What?" I asked Whhat.

We sailed toward the island in the distance and were greeted by an enchanting young creature with rainbow-thread hair. Before I could ask her *why in the world we were here in the world*, she smiled, as if already knowing what we had come for.

"Fun," was all she said, as she handed us each a swathe of fairy floss and danced us into her world.

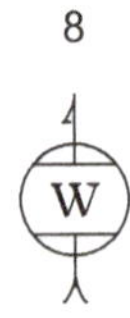

Madame
Pica Whiplashia

THE ISLAND OF
FUN

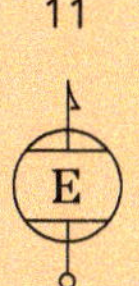

The Island of Fun was settled in 9874637481 by an escaped convict, Emippa Valdezfez. Emippa was locked up for a prank call she made on a powerful businessman and was sentenced to life in prison. She had spent most of her long life witnessing a lot of mindless suffering until one day she made a run for it, she jumped over the fence, stole the first boat she could find and sailed away. She discovered this small abandoned island and invited all the clowns in the world to come and make a home with her here. Everyone on the island believes we are here to have as much fun as we possibly can, everyday.

You need never have another bad day for as long as you live.

CURRENT RULER

Madame Piawhiplashia

MOON PHASES

Always, sometimes, never.

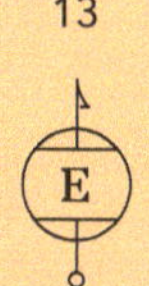

CURRENCY

Almond Croissants

EXPORTS

Decks of cards, hula hoops, roller-skates, badminton rackets, costumes and coconuts.

ATTRACTIONS

The Underwater-Waterfall Parks

INSTITUTIONS

The University of Silver-Lined-Clouds

RENOWED SUBJECTS OF STUDY
How to turn everyday into a Sunday.
The world-wide history of jokes.
The evolution of the finest prank calls.

THE LAW

No crying, no gambling, no bedtimes, no prisons and no coffee.

Madame Piawhiplashia
RULER
FLAG
↑ FLAG

INSTITUTIONS
MOON PHASES
ATTRACTIONS
Always
Never
Sometimes
The University of Silver Lined Clouds
The Underwater Waterfall Parks

Now during our time on the island of Fun we simply had had the time of our lives. When it was time to go we re-boarded our raft and were satisfied that why we were here in the world, was to have fun. With everything settled in our minds, we began our journey back home. But on the way, we got lost. Soon we were fast approaching another island, where we were greeted by a man with a wild green grin and a clipboard.

"No, no, no. You have it all wrong. Progress my dears! Progress is the real reason why we are here," and he whizzed us onto his island in his fancy solar-powered golf cart.

THE ISLAND OF
PROGRESS

The largest island of the oceans has been in the business of accumulating knowledge for as long as anyone can remember. The land is covered in libraries that stretch hundreds of stories into the sky and hundreds of stories beneath the ground. The history of the island itself is stored in bookshelves so far underground that no one knows where it is anymore. Everyone on the island believes we are here to discover more and more, everyday.

One day we will know the truth.

CURRENT RULER

Roberto Robertson-Roberts

MOON PHASES

Infinite

CURRENCY

Essays

EXPORTS

Telescopes, microscopes, rockets, planets and atoms.

ATTRACTIONS

The Staircase to the Stars

INSTITUTIONS

The University of Non-Absolute Truths

RENOWED SUBJECTS OF STUDY
The never-endingness of numbers.
The art of making-up new words.
'The more you know, the less you know' and other myths.

THE LAW

No conclusions, no destinations, no slacking off and no sleep.

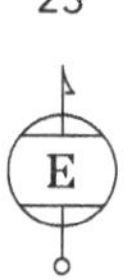

FLAG
INSTITUTIONS
EXPORTS

"Well that does seem to make more sense," I noted as we climbed aboard our raft once more.

"What?" asked Whhat.

"Progress. It just makes sense. It's awfully sensible and makes terrible sense. Doesn't it?" I said firmly.

Whhat frowned, unconvinced.

We were deep in thought, silently weighing up the pros and cons of the two very different islands, when we suddenly hit another island. A grey creature on stilts walked out into the ocean and dragged our raft to the beach with her bare hands. She helped us safely onto the sand and gave us both a mandarin juice in jars with the word LOVE handwritten on each of them.

29

THE ISLAND OF
LOVE

A group of five orphaned marsupials were left shipwrecked on the Island of Love back in 7834635267 during a violent storm. They all lost their parents in the weather and as a result they were grateful that they all still had each other. They vowed to never take their love for one another for granted and so they set up a new life on the Island of Love. Everyone on the island believes that we are here to love each other, everyday.

Kindness never runs out

CURRENT RULER

Harmoni Celeste

MOON PHASES

Saturday-Hatterday-Chatterday

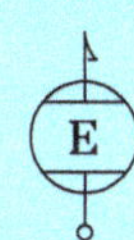

CURRENCY

Violets

EXPORTS

Wishes, Understandings and Acceptances.

ATTRACTIONS

The Museum of The Great Differences Between Everyone.

INSTITUTIONS

The School of Empathy

RENOWED SUBJECTS OF STUDY
How to understand anyone by listening to their story. Trusting your own choices. How to not compare.

THE LAW

Never, ever, ever be mean.

KINDNESS
NEVER
RUNS
OUT.
love

WHY IN THE WORLD ARE WE HERE
RULER

WHY IN THE WORLD ARE WE HERE
↓ FLAG

NDESS
VER
NS
UT.
love

"I love it there. That must certainly be *the* meaning of life, I'm totally convinced. Let's go home." I marvelled and clapped as I pushed the raft out into the water.

Again Whhat frowned and shrugged but I ignored her. And soon enough we saw another island on the horizon. A woman with tiny megaphones for eyes waved to us, beckoning us toward her. She was wearing a T-shirt that read: *I don't believe in artists.*

"Everyone makes something," her megaphones eyes echoed one after the other, as we climbed up the fairy-light harbour staircase.

45

E

THE ISLAND OF
CREATION

The Island of creation was created in 8765636536 by Pearl Siobhan. Pearl didn't like any other place there was in the world and so she decided to make her own land from scratch. She practiced building small islands in ponds and lakes before eventually taking on her big project in the middle of the sea. Everyone mad enough to believe in her came along with her and so from there they created their own way of being. Everyone on the island believes that the reason we are here in the world is to make up a reason for creating a reason.

Chase your wildest dreams

CURRENT RULER

Sylvester
Sylvia Sykes

MOON PHASES

Far off
someplace else

49

E

CURRENCY

Things

EXPORTS

Art, contraptions,
films and
plastic bags.

ATTRACTIONS

The Department Store
of Absolutely Every-
thing

INSTITUTIONS

The Believe-It and
Make-It School

RENOWED SUBJECTS OF STUDY
Deciding what to be when you grow up.
Having no fear.
The purpose of your creation.

THE LAW

No procrastinating,
no fear of failure,
no giving up.

OBSERVATION IS ONE OF THE MOST POPULAR ACTIVITIES IN THIS ISLAND.

CURRENT RULER: SYLVESTER SYLVIA SYKES.

SHOP OF ABSOLUTE E

WATER LEVITATION
EXPERIMENTS

BUILDING ONE OF THE ISLAND'S FIRST MOUNTAINS
SOURCE: HISTORICAL ARCHIVE
PEOPLE USUALLY DESIGN THEIR OWN HOUSES.
FLAG WAVING
TYPICAL DRINKS & FOOD.
ING
FILMING A NEVER ENDING FILM

"Well now I'm really confused," I mumbled as we set back out to sea. "Everything seems to make sense, and so I don't know which one to believe."

Whhat looked away from me.

"I wish you would say something constructive!"
I snapped at her.

Whhat didn't answer.

Days passed, and just when we thought we were permanently lost, our raft suddenly thumped against an empty looking land.

I thought I saw someone, but then again, I thought I didn't.

THE ISLAND OF
NOTHING

Nothing much has been written about the Island of Nothing because nothing much happens. Rumour has it, there was nothing here to begin with and there may even be nothing here now. Everyone on the island— if indeed there really is anyone there —believes that there is no reason why we are here.

Be

CURRENT RULER

No one

MOON PHASES

Unknown

CURRENCY

Everything is free, because there is not much

EXPORTS

Nothing

ATTRACTIONS

Nothing

INSTITUTIONS

None

THE LAW

None

NO-ONE

RULER
NO-ONE

MOTTO

0
0
FREE
0
0
EVERYTHING IS FREE, BECAUSE THERE IS NOT MUCH

CURRENCY

We returned quietly to our raft. We were silent as we rocked on the waves. A calm truth enveloped us. But of course, shortly thereafter we were distracted by the sight of a new land. A young girl waved a red flag from the shore, but then she disappeared and a peacock waved a yellow flag. Soon a crowd gathered and started bickering over the colours of flags, then they all dropped the flags and started singing. By the time Whhat and I had reached the shore everyone was melting marshmallows and speaking in several different languages.

THE ISLAND OF
NOW

The history for this island has been returned to the sky. They let everyday float away into the universe during sunset. Everyone is constantly changing their mind about everything. Everyone on the island believes that the reason we are here in the world is whatever reason you believe right now.

70

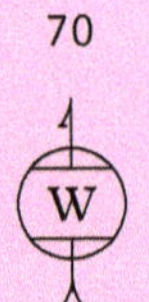

Moment to Moment

CURRENT RULER

~~Bob~~. We are just changing rulers right this very second.

MOON PHASES

When it rains

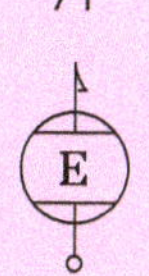

CURRENCY

Timepieces

EXPORTS

~~Distractions~~, non-distractions, meditations, levitations.

ATTRACTIONS

~~The Ever-Changing Railroad, The Technicolor Rain.~~ The Sunset Ceremonies

INSTITUTIONS

The Be A Different Person Everyday Institute

RENOWED SUBJECTS OF STUDY
Creating Costumes. Embracing Ageing. Changing Your Mind.

THE LAW

No thinking too much, no getting stuck in a rut, no holding on to the past.

3. RULER

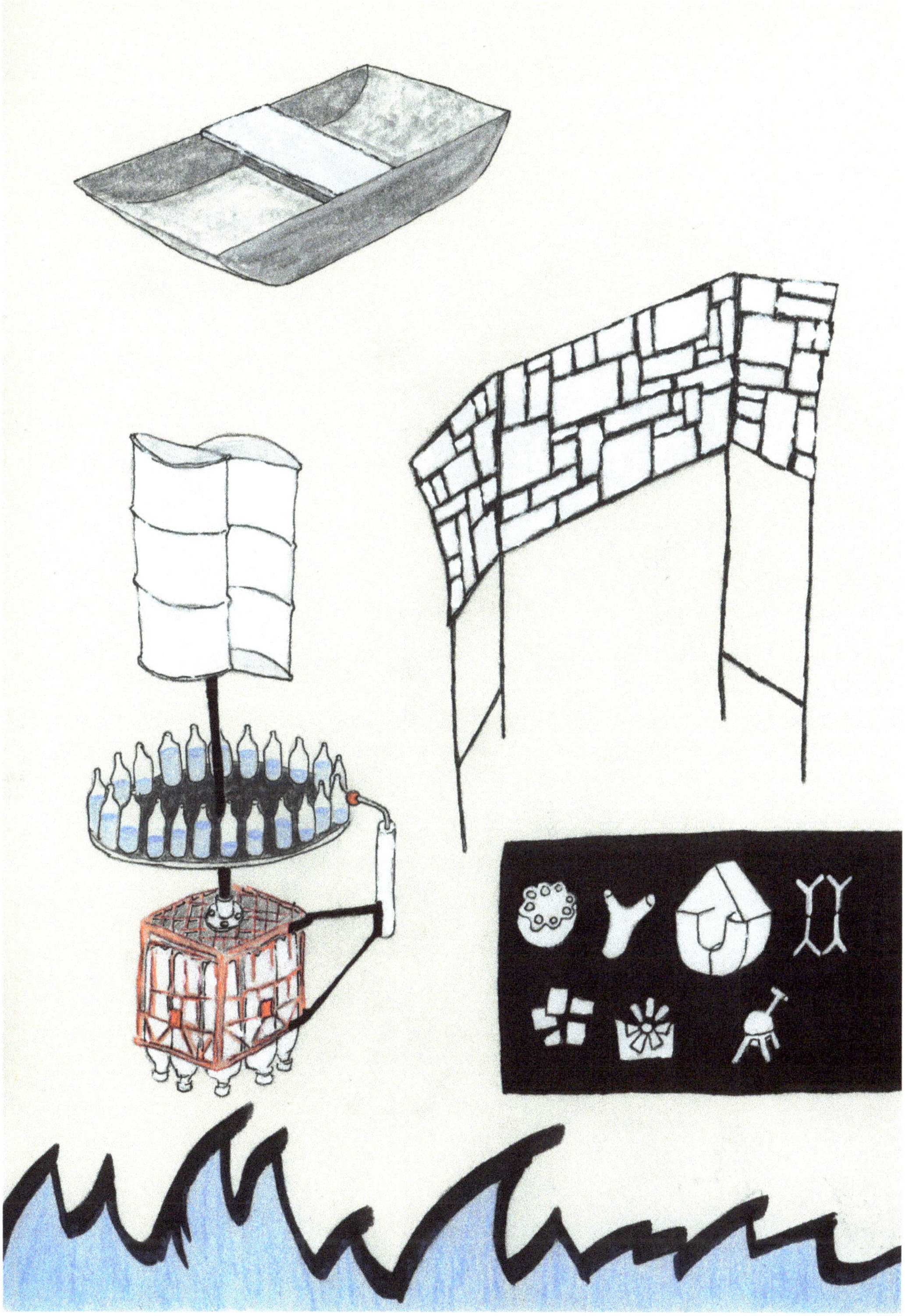

"Now that really sums it up perfectly, don't you think?"
I eagerly chomped down a marshmallow as I kicked back
in the sun.

"I JUST WANT TO GO BACK TO THE ISLAND OF FUN,"
Whhat barked hysterically, startling both of us and rocking
our raft.

But before we could argue over the details, we had been
lassoed by a long rope. Our raft was getting pulled towards
a giant, dark island. A cackling queen stood tall on some
jagged rocks, pulling us in our roped raft toward her.

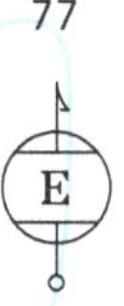

ISLAND

F POWER

Long before it was the Island of Power, this little island was the Island of Anything is Possible. So many mysteries, unexplainable happenings and magical chaos occurred that one day the King at the time lost his mind. The uncontrollableness of everything made him severely uncomfortable and so he re-instated a way of being that was much more practical and one that left no room for error. Everyone on the island is more at peace, the more in control they feel they are. They all believe we are here to rule the world.

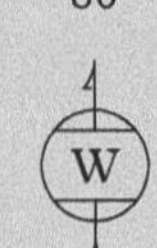

Winners are grinners, and losers fight in the carpark afterwards.

CURRENT RULER

Shakalacka Phire

MOON PHASES

Ask the moon

CURRENCY

Discipline

EXPORTS

Weather protection, locks, straight-jackets and traffic lights.

ATTRACTIONS

The Tower of Convincing Anyone of Anything.

INSTITUTIONS

The University of How Life Should Be Lived

RENOWED SUBJECTS OF STUDY

Why we must take control of this wild world. How power always goes to those who stop at nothing to get it. Why it is so important to be right and safe.

THE LAW

No disobeying anything, no new ideas, no risk-taking.

NO DISOBEYING ANY
NO RISK
WINNERS ARE GRINN
IN THE CARPA

IING, NO NEW IDEAS,
TAKING.
S, AND LOSERS FIGHT
AFTERWARDS.

ISLAND

F POWER

"Glorious, simply glorious" I sighed and shook my head in sheer appreciation. But Whhat was ignoring me, busy beginning to draw herself some kind of map, trying desperately to find a way to retrace our steps to the island of Fun no doubt. The ringing of ancient bells caused us both to look to the sky. We could see the sound in waves that flew above the ocean. The sound waves pulled us toward a mountainous land that crashed with sensations that we could see, touch, taste, smell and hear all at once. An old, familiar set of eyes reached out to me through the puzzling moment. An elderly blue man helped us onto the island. He held our hands as we walked.

THE ISLAND OF
DESTRUCTION

A mean old man who used to be called Zest found a splinter of a crystal a long time ago on a staircase on an island called Ashtertwinkle. The crystal was magic and Zest subsequently lived forevermore. However his body and mind changed over time and he began to go mad. The blinding beauty of the world was too much for him to bear. He could never explain why. He found this island full of creatures who could not be touched by the love of a rose. They found deep meaning in the company of each other. Zest changed his name to Apeirophobiac-Thanata-phobiahhhh-Rose. Everyone on the island believes that the reason we are here in the world is to destroy it, before its natural beauty fades, and they are left only with longing.

Why wait?

CURRENT RULER

Apeirophobiac-
Thanataphobiahhhh-Rose

MOON PHASES

Wish Wait Wonder
Why Who

CURRENCY

Poison

EXPORTS

Artificial Intelligence, Brain
Zaps, Sleeping Containers,
Dreams and Numbing
Agents.

ATTRACTIONS

The clifftop
walk amongst
the stars.

INSTITUTIONS

The University of
Mosquito-Zappers

RENOWED SUBJECTS OF STUDY
Discovering the passing of all things.
Questioning the worthiness of effort.
Accepting abysses.

THE LAW

Get smaller
every day.

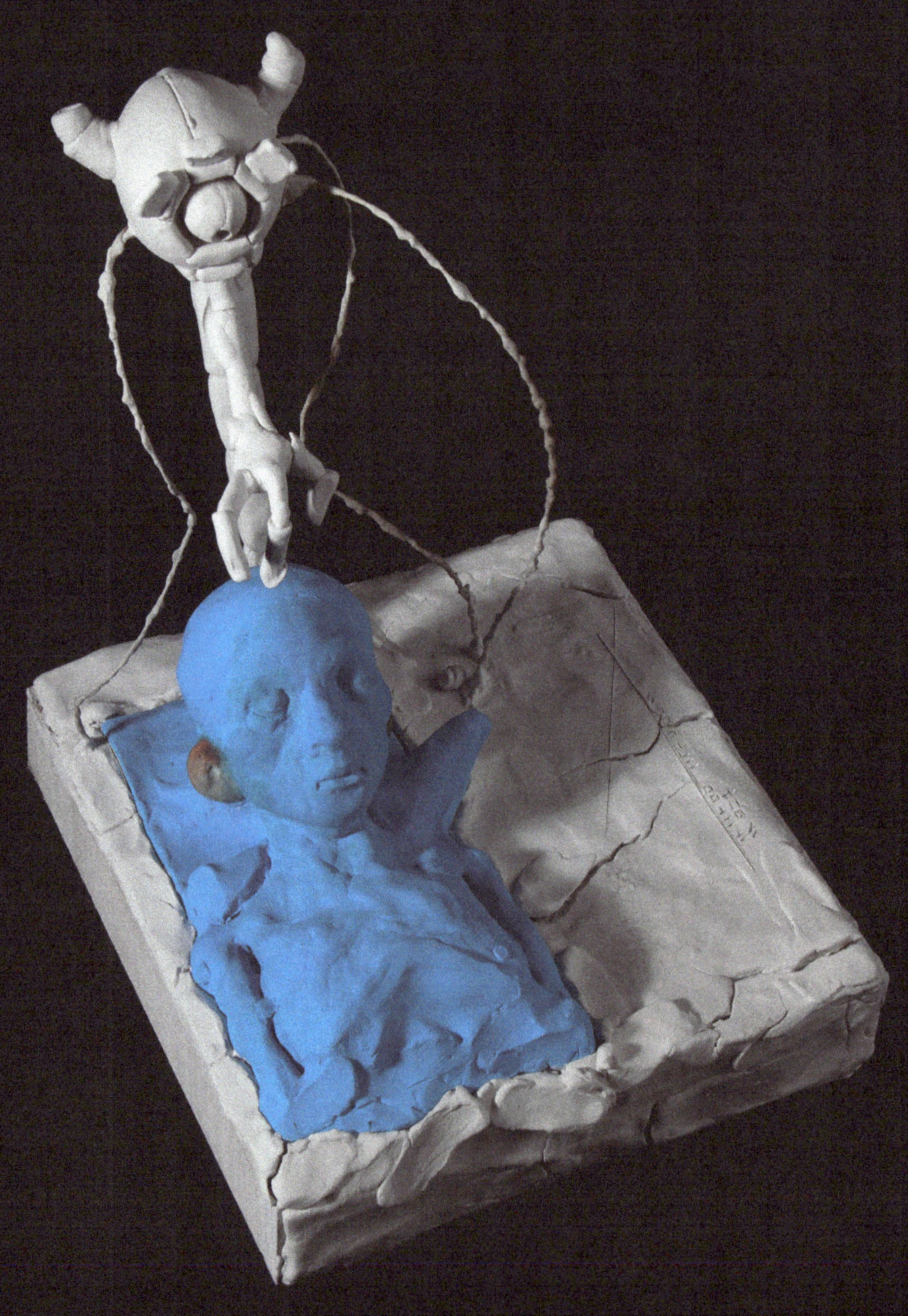
RULER

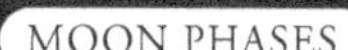
MOON PHASES

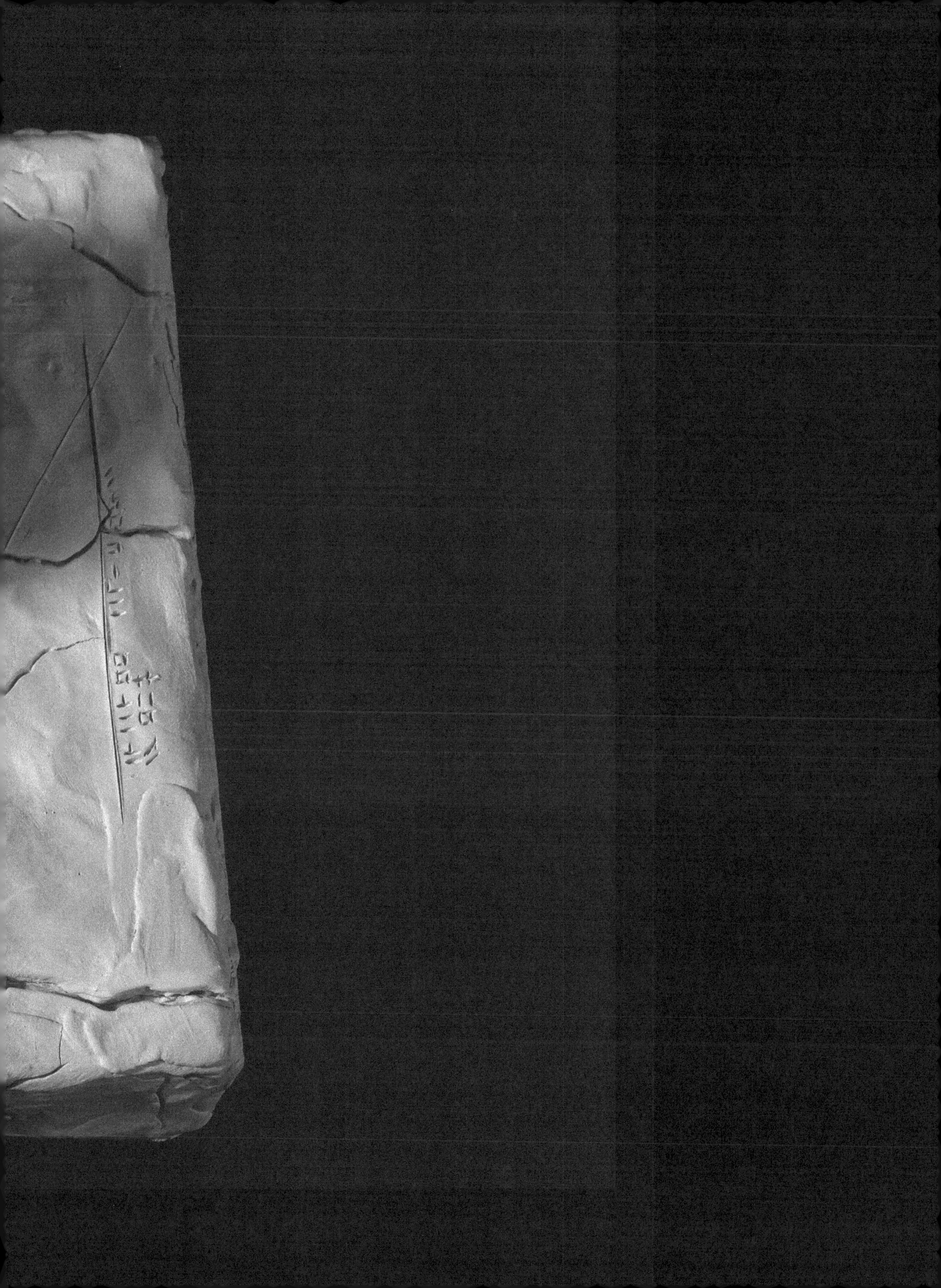

I felt a sadness and a love swell inside me. There was a genuine sense that an old scar had been healed but I did not speak to Whhat about it. In a matter of moments we were blinded by a bright light. Looking towards the light we saw a land made entirely of mirrors. There was a young girl's face grinning out at us from one mirror in particular.

"Hello," she purred, the soft echo of her voice ricocheting across the waves. We thought she was speaking to us, but she was actually speaking to another mirror, and then another one. We cautiously docked the raft and followed a chain of golden mirrors toward the sound of the girl's voice, I stopped briefly at one mirror to admire myself. I dusted a stray feather from my brow and then hurried to catch up with Whhat.

WORLD ARE WE HERE

THE ISLAND OF
ME

The Island of Me was founded in 76256738 by a renegade painter called Ghostwhorshiplia Carnivale. She believed the entire world was only a reflection and that to create changes she must work from the inside out. Ghostwhorshiplia spontaneously combusted when she was a hundred and one, and her ashes lit up the night sky in a firework so explosive that it could be seen from all over the world. This brought attention to her island and soon enough it became one of the most popular new places to live. Everyone on the island believes that they are in the world to bring out the best in each other.

Be the best you that you can be.

CURRENT RULER

Mia Miami

MOON PHASES

As the crow flies

CURRENCY

Quartz crystals

EXPORTS

Self-awareness books, blank journals, gym memberships and hairbrushes.

ATTRACTIONS

The Million Mile Mirror Maze

INSTITUTIONS

The Centre for Self-Discovery

RENOWED SUBJECTS OF STUDY
Venturing into the Endless Universe Inside.
Untangling My Thought Patterns.
Emotional Masterpieces.

THE LAW

No actors, no lying, no guilt, no catching butterflies.

SELF AWARENESS
export item: self-awareness book
flag
SELF AWARENESS

current ruler
export item: hairbrush

SELF
SELF
SELF
SELF
SELF-AWARENESS
export item: self-awareness book

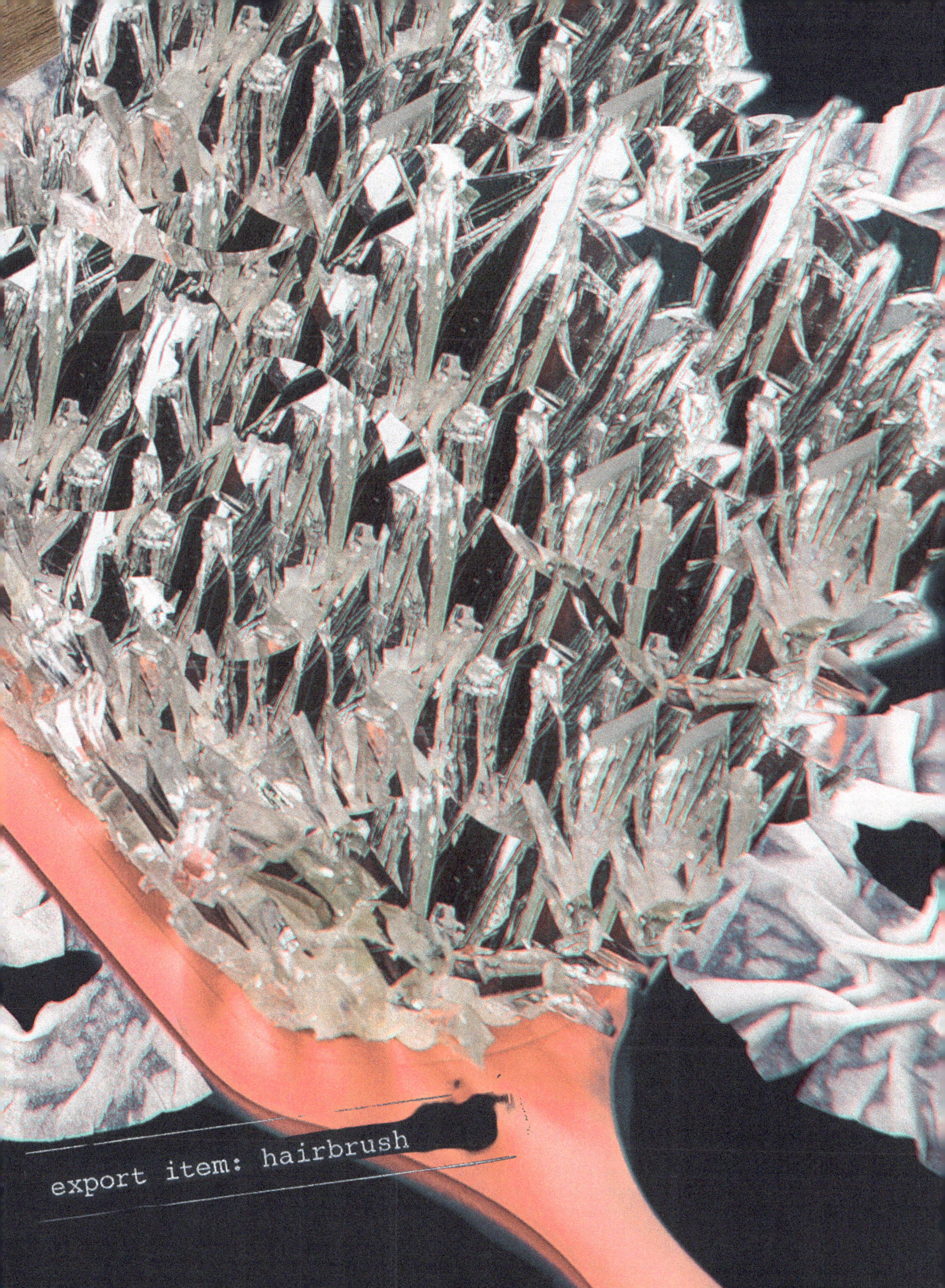
export item: hairbrush

WHY IN THE WORLD ARE WE HERE
export item: self-awareness book

current ruler

"It's quite self orientated isn't it?" Whhat mused when we found ourselves amongst the waters once more. "Like, if it was all about me, then why is there so many of us? Why isn't there just me? It's all so … *contradictory*, I mean why can't we just …"

I ignored her and instead tried to figure out why on earth there was suddenly a soft sphere of fiery energy igniting in my heart. I turned to see an island, with shadows of small creatures swirling in the clouds above it. A winged woman perched in a tree-top caught me eye as we got closer.

CUCKCOO

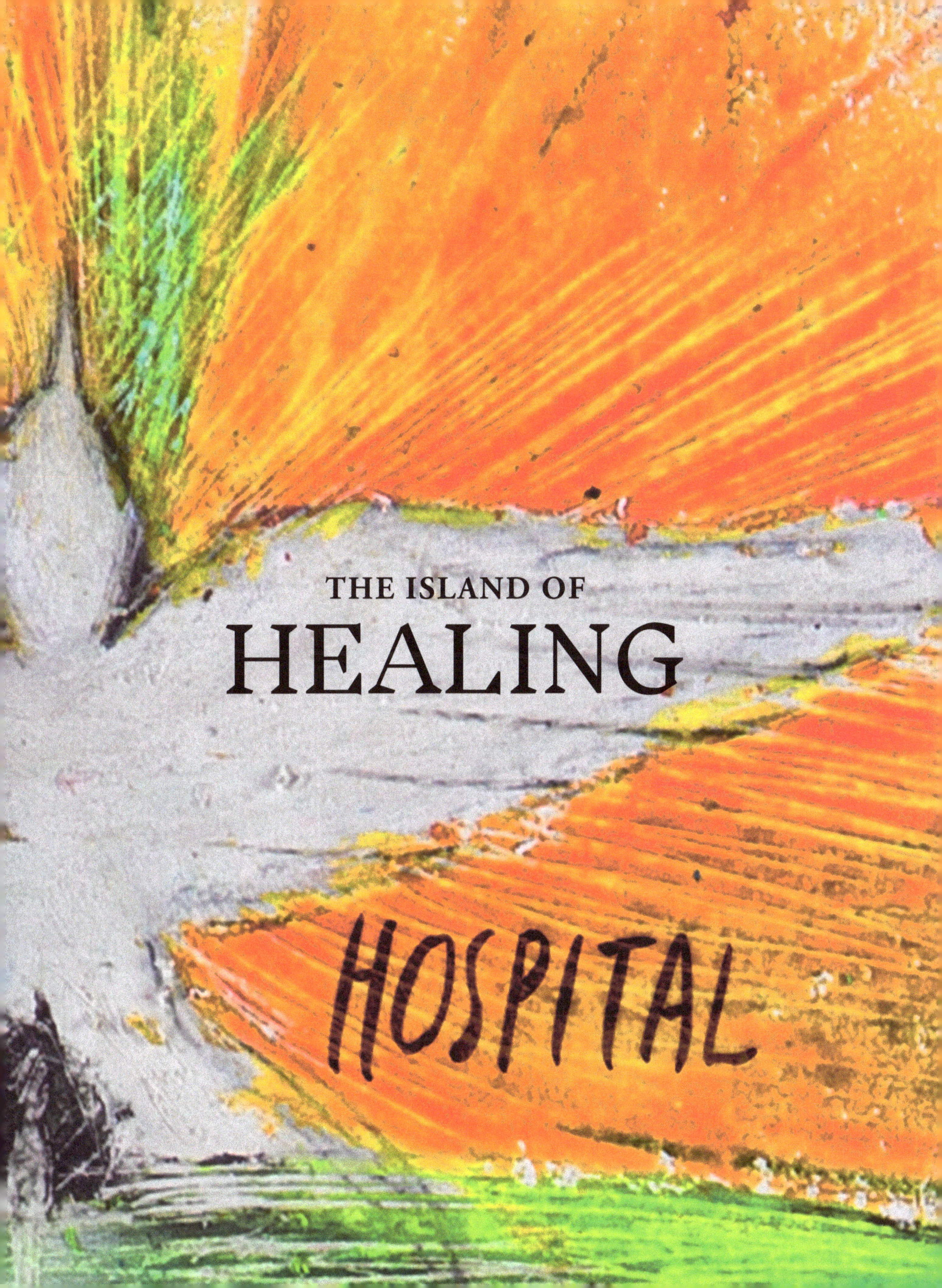

THE ISLAND OF
HEALING
HOSPITAL

The Island of Healing was discovered by two very sick people, Jing Jing and Norma. They had been on a life boat for eleven years and were initially thrilled to find land. The island was completely covered in birds, moths, insects and anything else that could fly. One of the moths told them that the island was the destiny of anyone who needed healing. Jing Jing 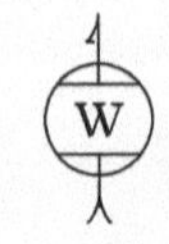 believed the moth and Norma did not. The next day Norma turned into a bat, and Jing Jing embarked on a three-hundred and fifty seven year journey of daily practices in order to heal. "Heal from what?" visitors to the island would often ask each other in the years that followed … "From life, from death, from eternity," the birds would always whisper.

Stop

CURRENT RULER

Jing Jing Wings

MOON PHASES

A little bit, change,
a little bit more, change,
keep going, repeat

CURRENCY

Acupuncture
needles

EXPORTS

Belief

ATTRACTIONS

The meadow
of stillness and the
eternal tent-lands
of strength.

INSTITUTIONS

One cuckoo hospital,
full of birds, a vast open
grasslands twinkling
with glittery feathers.

THE LAW

Heal another,
not just the one
who heals you.

THE MEADOW OF STILLNESS

INSTITUTIONS
CUCKOO
HOSPITAL
CURRENCY
ACUPUNCTURE
NEEDLES
NEEDLES
EXPORTS
BELIEF
MOTTO
STOP

THE LAW
HEAL ANOTHER NOT JUST THE ONE WHO HEALS YOU.
THE ISLAND OF HEALING WAS DISCOVERED BY TWO VERY SICK PEOPLE JING JING AND NORMA. THEY HAD BEEN ON A LIFE BOAT FOR ELEVEN YEARS AND WERE THRILLED TO FIND LAND. THE ISLAND COMPLETELY COVERED IN BIRDS, MOTHS
"HEAL FROM WHAT?" VISITORS TO THE ISLAND WOULD OFTEN ASK EACH OTHER IN THE YEARS THAT FOLLOWED... "FROM LIFE, FROM DEATH, FROM ETERNITY." THE BIRDS WOULD ALWAYS WHISPER
INSECTS, AND ANYTHING ELSE THAT COULD FLY. ONE OF THE MOTHS TOLD THEM THAT THE ISLAND WAS THE DESTINY OF ANYONE WHO NEEDED HEALING. JING JING BELIEVED THE MOTH AND NORMA DID NOT. THE NEXT DAY NORMA TURNED INTO A BAT, AND JING JING EMBARKED ON A THREE-HUNDRED AND FIFTY SEVEN YEAR JOURNEY OF DAILY PRACTICE IN ORDER TO HEAL.

By the time we got to our raft again, we were
both so exhausted that we fell asleep.
We drifted out into the ocean, both of us lost
in our dreamscapes.

When we woke, we saw the no-name creatures
swimming in the waters below.

And finally, we were home.

We looked at each other and then at our
beautiful glipperty-boomp island.

Beneath the moon-suns we thought and
thought and thought and thought, as confused
as we had always been.

122

Can <u>You</u> help Eia & <u>Whhat</u> create their Island's own identity & meaning?

WHAT DOES YOUR ISLAND LOOK LIKE?

WHAT DOES YOUR ISLAND LOOK LIKE?

NAME OF ISLAND AND BRIEF HISTORY

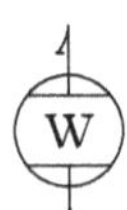

NAME OF ISLAND AND BRIEF HISTORY

CURRENT RULER

MOON PHASES

CURRENCY

EXPORTS

ATTRACTIONS

INSTITUTIONS

THE LAW

MOTTO

THE ARTISTS

Cassandra King
The Island of Fun

Cassandra is a Melbourne based Illustrator and Artist. Since completing a Diploma of Illustration and an Advanced Diploma of Creative Product Development at Melbourne Polytechnic, she has been freelancing and exhibiting work in local galleries. Her artmaking methods vary from traditional painting to digital rendering but mostly, her works are created by using thread, aged paper and painted scraps of fabric. This exploration of texture, pattern and the combination of various mediums is often her inspiration for making work. Cassandra uses embroidery as a form of drawing and painted material to create her collaged compositions.
instagram.com/cassandraking_7

Danica Chappell
The Island of Progress

Danica Chappell is a visual artist based in Melbourne who has a curiosity for spatial-temporal abstraction. Working with the elasticity of process from 'darkroom haptic' actions, Danica skirts the peripheries of photography to deconstruct material conventions. Danica completed her Masters of Fine Art (by Research) at Victorian College of the Arts in 2012. Danica exhibits regularly and her works are held in private and public collections, nationally and internationally.
www.danicachappell.com

Patrick Sluiter
The Island of Power

3D Designer and Animator based in Brooklyn, New York. Thoughtful, playful, and groovy are the building blocks to my work.
www.patricksluiter.myportfolio.com

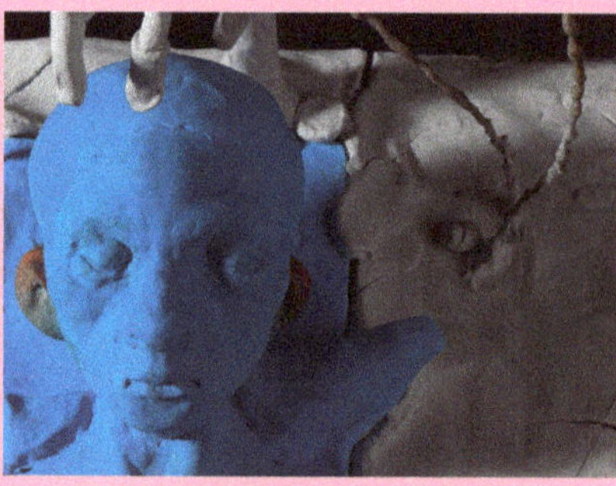

Alexander Esenarro Santafe
The Island of Destruction

Esenarro has been creating sculptures over the past 20 years, he has chosen ceramics as his medium for its unique beauty and strength. Esenarro is a citizen of the planet Earth and is based in Melbourne Australia since 2011.
www.esenarro.com

Honor Bradbeer
The Island of Love

Honor Bradbeer is a Melbourne-born artist and mother. She has been making, teaching, exhibiting or thinking about drawing for more than twenty years. She is named after her maternal grandmother, who was orphaned at the age of 3 while living on the island of Gibraltar in 1922. If it weren't for this awful tragedy, neither Honor junior, nor her sister, daughter, mother, aunts, uncle or cousins would ever have been born. So islands and orphans are pivotal to her story. And love is why she is here.
www.honorbradbeer.com

María Medem Pérez
The Island of Creation

www.mariamedem.tumblr.com

Antoine Nogueira
The Island of Nothing

www.behance.net/antoinenogueira

Emil Toonen
The Island of Now

Emil Toonen is a Melbourne based artist working with the manipulation of consumer detritus for creatively liberating outcomes.
www.emiltoonen.com

Yongho Moon
The Island of Me / The Island of Healing

Yongho Moon lived in South Korea before coming to Australia, He has many talents, including skills as an engineer, but his passion is contemporary arts and design. His work has been shown both in Australia and South Korea where his media art has been projected on the giant facade of Seoul Square. He loves collaborating with Clare who he says offers him the freedom to develop ideas in his own way.
www.yonghomoon.com

Why in the World Are We Here
Young Philosophers Series Vol. 3
A Whereabouts of Wanderings

Written by Clare-Rose
Editor Josey De Rossi
Design Futureinform

Published in 2023 by Red Wool Editions
Copyright © Clare-Rose and Futureinform 2023

ISBN 978-1-925864-37-3

Mailing Address
Red Wool Editions
PO BOX 8175 Subiaco East WA 6008
www.redwooleditions.com

Visit the Author's Website
www.clare-rose.com

The Young Philosophers Series
The Young Philosophers Series is intended as a place
children can explore philosophy by doing it, rather than
by being told about what it is and isn't.

At Red Wool Editions, we believe that children are natural
philosophers and so we have started our first series
exploring the complexities of oneself, contradiction, the
thoughts of others, change, the meaning of life and
senses of place. The books focus on the basic elements
of storytelling as we venture further into the universe of
your thoughts and eventually, your stories.

To find out more about philosophical journaling and
other books by Red Wool Editions visit clare-rose.com.
You'll also discover our upcoming theme park of activity
books that show you how to turn your wonderings into
your stories and how those stories may come to both
reflect and shape our spellbinding lives.

Red Wool Editions
Red Wool Editions is a publishing company dedicated to
unravelling the philosophical thoughts of kids, by taking
them through enchanting stories, twinkling soundtracks
and accompanying educational packages for parents
and teachers. Our aim is to encourage young readers to
create their own stories and open up family discussions
on how they want to live their life and why.

If you want to learn about forth-coming publications
subscribe to www.facebook.com/redwooleditions